A Hopeful Journey

Fight! Don't give up!
God Delivers on New Year's.

Written By
Hope Lajul

This is a Story of Healing…and God's Goodness

Dedication

This book is dedicated to God first and foremost for all his goodness and loving kindness that endure forever, his mercies that are new every morning! And for healing and life! I dedicate this book to my amazing son, darling, remember you are victorious! No weapon fashioned against you shall prosper in Jesus' mighty name. Always remember the goodness of God in your life, and never forget his benefits Psalm 103:1-5. Psalms 91 over you. To my lovely parents, Pastor Gabriel Lajul and Mom Pauline Lajul, you always taught us how to pray and to trust in God for everything. God bless you as you read. To my awesome siblings and all their spouses, may you always remember the goodness of God as you read.

And lastly, to all my wonderful readers! May this book bring you faith, hope, and Grace with many answers to your prayers, may you find a sense of peace as you read. I pray that God grants you all your heart's desires, and may you be amazed at his goodness. I pray that you are blessed, and may God's will be done in your lives as you find healing in all spheres of life as you read this book in Jesus' name. Amen Psalm 118:17

Acknowledgement

I would like to thank God so much for how far he has brought us. To everyone who played a role in my and my son's journey in one way or another, by praying or supporting financially or just by words of encouragement. Thank you

To my Dad, pastor Gabriel Lajul, and Mom, Pauline Lajul, you are the best! I don't know what I would have done without you. May God bless you abundantly.

To all my lovely siblings: Faith, Grace, Pastor Emmanuel, Gideon, Moses and Daniel and their spouses. You guys are the best. What would we have done without your support in many ways!

My son's father, who played a big role in many ways, thanks! This story wouldn't be here without him. And thank you to Papa Amaza, my father-in-law, for all the support and help.

Mom Ammie Patrick, who was involved all through the process, she inspired me and prayed with me before I got married I told her, and she cautioned me, mom prays for me and my son every day, God bless you mom we love you.

My Aunt Alice, who was involved in my journey from the word go. God bless you so much!

Pastor Thomson, Mama Grace, all their children, the word encounter church at large, thank you for all the prayers, encouragement, and all forms of support.

Brother Shadrack, who played a big role in my son's first steps to school in America, and also visited us in the hospital in Uganda when my son was just born, and he prayed for him and said they would play soccer together someday in America we didn't even know we would travel at the time, a couple of weeks ago he saw my son and he is a big boy now. Mama Darnell and Papa Darnell, Mariam, and Simon, who were a source of encouragement. Pastor Superior and Mom Joy, thank you for all the prayers and care.

Aunt Pam and her lovely children, Uncle Ram and Isaac, thank you.

Pastor Peter and Margo, and the church at large in New York, Pastor Shane, Wendy, and all the church at large.

Pastor/dad Micheal and Mom Vicky for always being there and the support in all ways.

Pastor Joe and Mama Sia, all their children and the OFM New Jersey 1 church at large for all the prayers and support. Apostle Jhonson Suleman, such an encouragement! Thank you for all the prayers.

Sister Mabel, Julie, and her amazing family, thank you.

Pastor Phil Chorlian, who encourages and prays for us, Pastor Charles Taylor, for the prayers, inspiration, and the spiritual guidance, Pastor Mary Anne de la Torre, kids church, and all the pastors at the vineyard church. Thank you.

To all my sons' teachers, all our friends and family that I can't mention one by one. You know yourselves! Thank you so much.

We love each one of you.

Enjoy reading!

Table of Contents

Struggles with Pregnancy

A few months after my wedding, I found out I was pregnant, and we were very excited as this sparked joy in our hearts. Marriage; we all looked forward to having our baby, and I did everything right: went to all my doctors' visits, took all my multivitamins, ate the best way I could, and rested to my best.

Suddenly, one morning, I started cramping. The pain was on and off at first, and I thought it was a normal pain, but then it worsened and progressed. Being alone at home, I picked up my phone and called my mom. She said, "Let's pray, and then you go to the hospital right away. I will find you there." My mom's voice was stern, the tone she only uses when there's a problem.

I rushed to the hospital, but a sad feeling gripped me. I sensed that something was wrong. The pain was not normal, and I was only 12 weeks pregnant!

Well, I made it to the hospital with my driver's help and went straight to the emergency room. After one nurse examined me, I was surrounded by many other nurses and doctors. They murmured and seemed unhappy, speaking in their medical terms, and all I could gather was, "Hope, you and the baby might be in trouble."

Finally, one doctor came over and said, "Mom, you are having a miscarriage." I can't forget the face of that doctor that gave me the news.

While shaking and crying, I inquired if there was a way to save the baby. They looked at me with a "less hopeful kind of face" and said, "We will try our best," and they did try, but the baby couldn't make it... he was a boy. The pain I went through was immense. Emotionally, mentally, and physically, I was a wreck.

I had my lovely parents by my side all through. They lived in a different town, 3 hours away from my marital home, and as soon as I told them about the pain, both Mom and Dad said, "Call your doctor, go to the hospital," then they started driving to me. They came straight to the hospital, and the whole time they were with me in the process. They held me, prayed for me, and hugged me. All my family gave me the support I needed. God bless you, Mom and Dad. My husband was away, but he came back and stayed with me during this time. He didn't know what to do, and he was sad as well.

After that painful miscarriage, we both couldn't heal mentally and emotionally. There was this huge hole in my heart. The longing for a baby in my arms was consuming me, and nothing could fill that gap other than a baby. Every time I saw any mom carrying a little baby, I smiled with them, hiding my deep-seated sadness and longing to hold my own baby someday. I wish I hadn't had a miscarriage. I would be holding my own son now.

This escalated the problems I was already having in my marriage. My husband started staying away, and he struggled with the loss, too. He had long bar nights, came home drunk at weird hours of the night, and sometimes spent nights away in places I didn't know. He always complained that he married me and did everything right, but I couldn't give him a baby. We fought more, the disconnect increased, he stopped caring, and this was the last thing I needed. I became more worried and cried severely. I would cry myself to sleep every night. Depression and loneliness stepped in.

Praying and Surrendering

I turned to God, and I have always been a believer. Dad and Mom raised us in church. However, I hadn't sought God personally as I did this time round. My safe haven was in worship, and I was crying to God. I prayed always, went to church, and read my Bible.

One year after that miscarriage, despite trying to get pregnant and praying for a baby and testing several times with negative results, my husband says to me, "Why can't you get pregnant?" I say, "I don't know, maybe you should be home more, work on your drinking, let's pray more." He snaps and says, "Really? It's you with problems. Get pregnant. This is on you, Hope."

I didn't even know him anymore. We were like strangers again. My crying to God and talking to Mom and my sisters helped me deal with the pain, but he was dealing with his pain differently. We struggled and lost the initial fire we had for one another.

But that month, when we talked and I said try to stay home more, he heard me, and I kept on praying, touching my tummy daily, saying I am pregnant (speaking into existence what is not there, as the scripture says in Proverbs 30:32, to speak life to every situation). I prayed and fasted, and my sister-in-law said to me, "Hope, stop fasting, eat well, eat lots of avocados and healthy meals that your heart desires, and quit worrying." So I did that as I kept on praying and just thanking God for my situation.

Just a few weeks into doing that, as I was going about my business, I realized I was feeling a certain way and just an overall feeling of exhaustion and tiredness, as I had been waiting for a whole year to get pregnant. I thought, hmm, why not check again and see? And this was not the first time I had checked for pregnancy. Most of my tests were negative, and all the symptoms just turned out to be my periods.

So, I hesitantly picked up a test kit. I bought a lot of them, and looking at the test kit, anxiety and worry of not seeing two lines swept over me. "Should I waste this one again?" I asked myself. Hmm... it always gives me negative answers anyway, despite my feeling a certain way, which I thought was my period... I walked to the bathroom to take the test, and as soon as I did it, I looked away because I didn't want to keep my eyes on it. I didn't want to see the test be negative. I looked away and started singing just to help me set my expectations in the right place.

A few minutes passed, and I looked at the test kit. It had two lines... two lines! Whattt! I couldn't believe my eyes... I picked it up and looked closely again just so I was sure this was a positive test, to be certain it was not going to change again to one line... I was nervous. After looking closely, I saw that there were still two lines. I smiled, got the test kit, and came to a brighter light so I could look closely, and it still was two lines. I shouted, "Thank you, Jesus!" Rolled on the floor and just kept thanking Jesus for the positive pregnancy test.

Something that I had waited and prayed for and had one-on-one talks with God about had just happened. Amen!

My husband wasn't home that day. I couldn't wait to tell someone the news, so I called his phone—no answer. I called Mom, and she answered immediately, and I told her (Mommy and my sisters Grace and Faith prayed with me all the time, and they were always on the phone).

She shouted, "Oh, thank you, Jesus!" She jumped and danced, and we all celebrated, thanking God for the answered prayer.

The Journey Through Pregnancy Again

Knowing I was pregnant was the best feeling ever. I felt happier, and the fights between me and my husband reduced. My love for God increased, and indeed, knowing God keeps his promises to us kept me more tuned to relying on him more than anything and everything I was doing.

In the first trimester, I struggled a lot, didn't like to eat, and threw up a lot. I got ill with malaria, which was bad during pregnancy, and I was in and out of the hospital always.

My Mommy and sisters, Grace and Faith, prayed with me all the time, and they were always available to talk and listen to me when I needed them on the phone. My husband was not there; all of the hospital visits, I was alone.

I realized despite being pregnant, the damage to my marriage was already done. This man had changed and probably had other priorities that weren't me anymore and that came first. There was still that loneliness, but being pregnant always gave me a smile. I got really weak, and I pulled through with the help of God. I made sure I did all the doctor's visits and had all my vitamins, which I took as per the doctor's directions.

As I was approaching my second trimester, the doctor asked me to be on bed rest, just so I was not at any risk with the baby. So I resigned from my job and moved to my other home in the city close to a good hospital and my Gyn.

My tummy kept growing, and I did well in the second trimester, throwing up less. I actually only enjoyed not feeling super sick at this stage.

I had ample rest, but my husband was never home. He could go away on work trips for weeks or a whole month, and I wouldn't see him. Communication was dwindling, maybe twice a week with brief talks, or sometimes more times a week, but not every day.

In my third trimester, my husband and I fought a lot (verbally). I was drained in many ways. He was struggling too; he didn't talk much about his struggles, and he resorted to drinking and the bar.

One day, as we were driving home early in the morning from a friend's wedding party, he got into a huge fight, so I got out of the car to try and stop him, and he gave me a good slap. The fight escalated, and it was going to be so bad we both could have ended up spending the night locked up as he was drunk driving. But I went to the car and cried out to God to end this scuffle. I was so stressed out. This incident was the worst. Remember, I am pregnant. My belly was now noticeable. I was 30 weeks pregnant at the time. Later, we managed to get out, and as soon as we got home, he yelled and insulted me more, which made me so sad. I cried so much, and then I was thankful to God we got home safely.

But that took a toll on me. I started feeling unwell right after that. A week went by, and my husband traveled away for his work trip. I was still unwell, so I went to see the GYN for scans, and everything seemed well.

However, I still continued feeling off. I had this on-and-off cramping, which just couldn't go away. A day before my husband had traveled, the pain got worse, and it was late at night. I was home

6

alone at 1 a.m., I called him, and he said he would come. I waited for hours, but he wasn't home, so I called the security guard who worked the night shift to help me get to the health center. Later, my husband found me there, and then my family came. I spent that night and many other nights there, stayed there for a few days, and before I could go back home, my husband traveled out of the country, leaving me in that state.

However, the gynecologist in this health center referred me to my main Gyn/doctor in a bigger hospital, and immediately, my big brother came around. He drove me there, and we went straight to the ER. Before I knew it, I was surrounded by nurses and doctors. Remember, I am 32 weeks pregnant now. I hadn't prepared anything for having a baby; I had no clothes, no sheets, and nothing.

When the doctors examined me, they said to me, "Hope, the baby is coming. You are having a baby today." After hearing this, I had mixed emotions. I was happy that I would see my baby and carry him, but super sad and nervous because I knew he wasn't due. Also, I wasn't ready mentally, and I just wasn't sure all was well, having had a bad experience before. However, I was excited to be a mom. I looked up to God, and he was with me at that moment. Mom and Dad were far away in another city, but God was right in this moment with me, right here with me, and my big brother, who is a pastor, was with me. He didn't live in my city at the time; he had come in for an errand, and he stopped by to visit me. But God brought him divinely when I needed all the support. My brother Emmanuel held my hands and prayed with me. He spoke life into this situation, and he encouraged me that all would be well.

We checked into the room, and I wasn't sure how to feel. All I knew was I was scared, worried, nervous, and hungry. I hadn't eaten for days, so my brother went to get me food and to buy baby clothes, and as soon as he went out the door, the doctor came by and said,

"Hey, Hope, because we don't want to take any risks, the scan results show that the baby has the umbilical cord around his neck, we have to have you go for a C-section, and we will take the baby to the NICU as soon as he is delivered..." NICU???? What's that? It gave me anxiety, but he said my child is safer in the NICU (Nursery for premies) since he is considered a preemie. "At 32 weeks (technically, he should be 38–40 weeks to be safe), we will pick you up as soon as the nurses prepare you. Do not eat anything, ok?" This doctor was a family doctor, and he was kind to us; he knew my struggle from the beginning.

I cried more, got more nervous and worried, and got lost in my thoughts. I said, God, please keep me close, embrace me and hold my hands, engulf me in your bosom. May I not be in any trouble with my son; keep us safe, please God.

As soon as my brother came back in, I told him I couldn't eat the food, and the doctor came back and explained everything to him again, and he was calm. He said, "Hope, be strong. God is in control. He has got you in his palms, he has great plans for you and your son, all will be well." He held my hands again and prayed with me. I had another lady helping me as well.

I was rolled off to the operating room, and Jesus was right there with me. I sensed his presence right with me. He held my hands and comforted me. I had so much peace. Despite everything, he said everything would be okay. So I surrendered to him at that point and relaxed. While the doctors and nurses were very nice and were doing a great job, talking to me and making sure I was okay, I imagined Jesus taking the wheel.

Wait Surprise!...My son is Born

While still caught up in my imagination, I heard the sweetest loud newborn baby cry ever. He came out strong, and that was my son. He was born. A couple of minutes later, the nurse showed him to me. He was so adorable, tall, and grown! He was strong with a loud cry. He was all I ever wanted. What an amazing experience! It blew me away. The nurse brought him to me, and I carried him for a little bit and said, "Baby, you are grown. Strong and highly blessed, I love you." And as soon as I spoke to him, he was whisked away from me. My brother was prepared by the nurses to hold him and speak to him, then take him to the NICU with the nurses, which he did.

I believe God sent big brother Emmanuel divinely to see this process. God will always make a way for us. You will never be caught up in a situation that's so bad, and God will not make a way for you, my friend. See 1 Corinthians 10:13. I am sure the devil meant bad, but God said despite the immature labor, I will make a way. Despite Hope's husband being away... I will send her brother, who is a pastor, so that he stands in the gap and is there as a strong spiritual and emotional support, to pray with us and just speak life and hope into the whole situation without judging or worrying. And what the devil meant for bad, God turns it for good. So focus on the good and don't cry for what's not there. That day, Mom and Dad drove up to be with me and to see their grandson.

As soon as he was born, I saw him briefly, blessed him, and

prayed for him. Then he was rushed to the NICU/Nursery, and the doctor said he didn't need to stay there long, maybe less than 2 weeks. He was strong, and his lungs were fully developed and didn't need surfactant.

After a couple of hours, I was brought back from the operating room to rest, and I didn't have my baby with me. I had to wait a day to see him, and that alone made me anxious. I wasn't whole until the day I went to see him. He was sleeping, but I gave him my finger, and he gave me a good grip! That was so relaxing. Despite not being with me, we had a way of connecting. So each time I came in, I gave him my fingers, and he held them until I left.

He had all these wires and monitors hooked around his bed and on his feet. I can't forget the beeping sound of these machines that check vitals.

He was tall, handsome, and happy. He only cried when he was hungry. He ate in bits, but after every 4 hours, he needed to be fed milk, which I expressed. Now, the children in the NICU are very delicate. Therefore, only the two parents are allowed to see their child, and they are highly sanitized before going to the NICU. You can't hold the baby in your clothes. You change your outfit and shoes at the entrance of the NICU, and they give you clean, disposable outfits to avoid any germs from spreading. Then you wash your hands and then go in. My husband wasn't there, so I went in with Mom, and she would pray for the baby and speak to him. She was very helpful. Dad would wait for us in the waiting room and beam when we came back, saying his grandson said hello.

I saw two parents (a dad and a mom) going to see their children in the NICU most of the time, and they clearly supported each other. However, I was always alone or with my mom. Some days, a different mom would break down, but her husband would be there to support her, hug her, or give her a shoulder to cry on.

But in my case, I had my tissues to blow my nose on if I was feeling down or thought about my situation. Thank God my Mom,

Dad, and siblings were there to stand with me.

Every day, I wake up and look forward to seeing my son. The pediatricians in the NICU were very dedicated and highly skilled, and the hygiene in the NICU was perfect.

I got updates on what was going on with him and his pounds, his height, his everything, and all was well.

The Battle with My Son's Health and Healing

Until one morning when I came in to see and feed my son, as I usually do. He was already a few days in the NICU, and he didn't seem as active as he was the previous night. He was cranky and cried a lot, so feeding him that day was a struggle. He seemed to be sleeping more. I stayed around for all my visits, as I was allowed 4 visits in a day. Each time I came in, I placed my hands on him and prayed over him. As I was about to leave, I prayed again and said goodnight, leaving a little sad and disturbed about the baby.

The following day, when I came in for my morning visit, the nurse called me and briefed me on my son's daily report. She said he was getting jaundiced, so they moved him to a blue light machine, and indeed, I didn't find my son in the same spot I had left him the previous night. He was moved to a different bed, and he had all these blue lights on him and glasses to protect his eyes from the light, so I got scared and worried again.

I couldn't feed him that day. The nurse fed him my expressed milk.

I prayed for him and surrendered to God, spoke the word of God over his life, 1 Peter 2:24, "By the stripes of Jesus we are healed," and I encouraged myself in the Lord.

I told my parents, sisters, and brothers, who also prayed for him.

I was still healing from the C-section and the fact that the baby was in the NICU and this jaundice! I needed him to be here and give me a hug… and just say, it's ok. Our son will be well. Or we will be well, don't fear, don't worry, I got you. But I was alone. I remember looking at 2 parents who always came in together to see their son at the NICU, and I missed my husband so much.

A tear rolled down my eyes as I walked to the waiting room. I waited for the next time to see my son. I cried so much in the waiting room. I heard the comforting voice of the Lord saying he was with my son and me. We are not alone, and this scripture, Psalms 23, clearly dropped in my mind. I started saying it out loud: Even though I walk through the valley of the shadow of death, I will fear no evil, for you are with me, Oh Lord.

Later that day, when I saw my son for my last visit, I spoke life in this situation. I said, "Son, you are healed, you are strong, and Jesus is with you." I held his little fingers, and he squeezed my hands right away, and I said, "I love you, baby. Mommy is here, and we got this! Jesus loves you." That was all I needed. I knew he heard me, and he was going to be well.

I was encouraged. I knew I had to shift my mindset, be strong for me and baby, and not break down.

I went back to my room, limping from the pain and stitches of the C-section. I had a long day, but I knew God was in control.

The following day, I saw my son still in the same blue light, but I was strong. I didn't cry, and I spoke life to his situation. I declared the word of the Lord over him, told him I loved him, he held my hands, and I held his, and that was all I needed. My husband was nowhere to be seen.

I stayed in my room for the rest of the day, as requested by my doctor, so I could heal and feel better too. Besides, I wasn't allowed to feed him yet while he was on the blue light treatment. The nurses fed him.

I saw my son for 2 more days and just kept praying over him, speaking life and the word of God in his situation. I told him, "Son, you are healed, you are strong, you will live and not die, Jesus is with you." He held my hand with a good grip, and that was all I needed for the day.

After staying for 4 days in the hospital, I was discharged to go back home. I lived close by, so I was going to be commuting back and forth to see my son in the NICU. I couldn't go back home with him, as much as I really wanted him close by with me.

Going back home without him was not easy. I remember telling Mom and the doctors that I couldn't leave the hospital. I wanted to be around my son, but they had to assure me that he would be okay. I needed to go home and recover too, as he recovers so that we all are ok. I really wanted to hold him.

Getting to my house without him was tough, but it gave me time to shop and arrange everything that I needed to do. Remember, he came when I wasn't ready. So we shopped and set up his crib with Mom.

The following morning, as they opened the NICU for parents to visit, I was the first there. More new babies had come in. One new baby was so tiny. She was only 26 weeks in her mother's womb, and then she was born. She was so small.

As I walked past her incubator towards my son's treatment room, I saw his nurse with a happy smile. She said, "He is out of the blue light." I was so excited to hear that! The nurse said his doctor wanted to see me.

So I went in, and the doctor was also smiling, and he said, "Most times, children stay under the blue light longer with the case he had, but your son has no symptoms. We wanted to be sure and run lab tests, and he is all ok," so we took him off the blue light. He is back to his regular bed so we monitor him, but he is doing great. You can go see him and feed him." All this while the doctor was talking, I was amazed at God's goodness! He had healed my son! I praised God so much, went and carried my son after many days, and fed him. He smiled and played more, and after I fed him, he tightly held my fingers and smiled. That was all I wanted to see. God is awesome. He answers prayers.

Days went by, and I kept on checking on him, praying for him to get out of the NICU and come home with Mommy as I patiently waited for him to reach the weight the doctors required before discharge.

After 2 weeks, I was expecting to go back home with him, but that morning, when I went to the hospital, the nurse said I had to see the doctor for my son's progress report.

That morning, I went in to meet the doctor, and she said, "Your son has sepsis." She said it's the little ones in the NICU who struggle with infections here and there as they are delicate.

So she put him on antibiotics, meaning we cannot go back home yet.

I looked at my boy, and he was not playing much and eating less, so I prayed for him and spoke God's word over that situation.

He was sick for a whole week, and by week 2, I still couldn't take him back home. I was expressing milk, and he wasn't drinking well. He lost some pounds.

After week 3, the doctor said we could go back home and monitor him and bring him back to the hospital for regular checks.

Now, I wasn't ready to have him home by myself. I had his crib ready, I just wasn't prepared mentally and emotionally. I had a C-section that wasn't healed yet. So my mom came and helped me get situated. We fixed his room and everything he needed. Life got tough because I had to step up. He needed extra care. I was up all day and night doing kangaroo, so he was nice and warm.

Regular feeding after every 4 hours, I had less sleep. Lots of sleepless nights and me crying, and Mom helping my son and me.

But one day, after he had been home for 2 weeks, I noticed he was pale and puffy. At first, I thought, was he gaining weight? We hadn't yet set up a nurse who could come home weekly for him. So, after a clear examination, I realized he was not looking well. That day, my mom and I rushed back to the hospital, panicking...

Illness Back to Back...

Moments later that day, after being examined by the doctors, they found out he was having heart failure symptoms, was very anemic, and was still not recovered from the sepsis he had gotten from the NICU two weeks ago. As a matter of fact, it had worsened. He was not gaining weight, he was not feeding well, and he was not sleeping well.

So, he was put on a heavy Myagel syrup (it's an antibiotic just for the tummy) and another antibiotic for children. Later, they discovered his heart rate was slow.

So, he was rushed in an ambulance to the heart specialist to examine his little heart (all this was happening around the same time. I was still sore from the C-section, and the fact that my husband was not here with us was tough, and I was getting postpartum depression).

Getting Savage on The Devil and The Best Way to Ride in An Ambulance

Now, in the ambulance, I decided to hold my son and sit with him on a different seat that's not for patients because he was little (you can still use the patients' seat). I think it's a caregiver seat. It's next to the patients' seat that I sat on with my son in my arms. At that moment, it is what you say that matters, so I kept saying, "Baby, you are healed! You are strong; you are going to live."

I got mad at the devil and started cursing it out of my son's life! My business and joy and my son's health! And my everything. I was pissed I had had sleepless nights, and my son had cried so much. Remember, the Bible tells us to resist the devil, and he will flee, so I kept declaring life into this situation. And the ambulance drove so fast with the siren and cars making way. I had never been driven so important like that, so I forged a smile and kept telling myself this is not a scary emergency (despite the circumstances). This is a VIP vehicle taking us, son, because we are VIPs. I didn't want to panic. I also made sure to cancel all the negative comments random people make when an ambulance is passing and there is someone fighting for their life in there.

And that helped me set the next tone at the heart hospital. I was composed and not worried. Of course, I was scared for my son, and I was under pressure. I didn't want anything bad to happen to him. I was alone there with him and his nurse. Then, soon, the specialist came and took us in. She examined him and heard a murmur, which showed a hole in the heart, and she showed me the screen. It was not a very small hole, and that's why my son was getting really sick.

The doctor said it's causing signs of heart failure, and if it doesn't dissolve in 3 months, then the baby will need an operation.

A Mother's Cry for Help

My heart sank. I didn't expect that news for my little one, especially by myself, while dealing with my crumbling marriage, my unhealed C-section, and the fact that I wasn't working due to a high-risk pregnancy, and I had no money.

Every mother needs a bathroom break alone…

At that moment, I held back a running tear and excused myself to go to the bathroom. Then, I cried like pouring rain. I cried to God for help! I was desperate…

I was a mess. I said, "God, please save my son. Save me from this whole situation. I need a miracle here. I don't want him to have any surgery. Please heal my son from all infirmity; all of them, Lord, have mercy on me. Forgive all my sins and his dad's sins. Remember this little one? I asked you for him, and you blessed me with him. Your word says the blessings of the Lord maketh rich and adds no sorrows to it! Lord, those are your words in the scripture, Proverbs 10:22, and you said, Lord, that children are an inheritance from the Lord in Psalms 127:3 and Exodus 23:26.

Lord, these are your words. Please make a way for my son. Remember your promises, Lord." When I finished crying to God, I turned to the devil.

Get Mad At the Devil!

I said, "Satan! You have no power over my son. In the name of Jesus, remove all your afflictions and claws off my child and my life! By the stripes of Jesus, my son is healed (1 Peter 2:24), so why are you still in his heart? In his body? Get out, Satan, now!" I was wild!! Here, listen to what this scripture says:

"But he was pierced for our transgressions, he was crushed for our inequities; the punishment that brought us peace was on him and by his wounds we are healed" (Isaiah 53:5)

That means that my son's healing has been paid for, and I demanded it! So, he—the devil—is a thief! After saying that to the devil with my proof of what the word of the Lord says about my son's healing and the exact spot in the Bible where it is located, I got out of the bathroom, still wild, and the nurse handed me my son. I looked into his eyes and told him, "Son, you are free! You are healed!" That moment, despite being so frail, he smiled back at me. I held his little finger, and he gave me a grip. I knew the next time we were coming back to the heart hospital, there would be a different result.

This is how Satan plays with your encouraged self. He makes the situation seem like it's not possible. Remember, as I was in the ambulance, I had encouraged myself in the Lord, so now, hearing the doctor's report, I was shaken, but in those moments, I turned to the word of God concerning that situation. Call for help from above, don't pity party, know your child needs you to fight for them.

So we went back to the hospital, still in an ambulance, and he was put straight on Lasix to help drain fluids from his heart and body. Meanwhile, he was also on antibiotics for the sepsis. He was also so pale, and he needed a transfusion at the same time.

He later started getting better, and from all of that, we ended up staying in the hospital for 2 months. He seemed to be on the right track. I was also getting rested but still had no husband around, and it was after Christmas. We actually had our 1st Christmas in the hospital as he was recovering and on all sorts of medication and monitoring. Everything seemed to be under control. He had started drinking more milk, but it was not adding weight, so his doctor prescribed a milk fortifier, which is added to underweight premies' diets just to boost his weight. It is heavy in milk protein, but I think it didn't do justice to my son's tummy, so after feeding him that for days consistently, my son seemed uncomfortable, but he looked ok. I couldn't put a finger on what was wrong after our daily review with the doctor that day of December 30th.

The New Year's Healing Miracle on Jan 1ˢᵗ

And having been in the hospital for more than 2 months, the doctor said we could go home and keep on medication and control at home, as my son was so much better. That was the best exciting news ever! We were to go home by December 31st, and we would be home in the new year.

However, early that morning on December 31st, my son started crying uncontrollably. I examined him and noticed his tummy was just so distended! I told the nurse, and they gave him anti-gas, Tylenol, and all sorts of pain relievers, but it didn't help.

He didn't stop crying. His tummy was still so tight, distended, and hard. With all the crying, the doctor had to examine him again, and he recommended an ultrasound for his tummy right away.

After looking at the ultrasound results, I could see the doctor panicking and struggling to say it to me. Remember, I am still postpartum, dealing with a bad marriage, and just tired of the hospital—all ready to go home—so I asked him, "Everything ok?" And he said, "No, he needs emergency surgery. He has an IO (Intestinal Obstruction)." I looked at my son again, and that's when it hit me that he had not been farting and hadn't pooped in a while!

I started panicking at that news again. I looked at my son, and he was still crying. He had cried until he didn't have any more tears.

He had a cannula in his little feet for treatment because all the veins in his hands were exhausted from pricks. He was looking so miserable and frail that I couldn't help him stop crying. Nothing was soothing him. He was in so much pain! They tried an enema, but it didn't work. Then, they inserted a tube into his tummy through his mouth to try and drain the substance in his tummy to reduce distension, but nothing came out at all.

The diagnosis was done in the morning at around 10 a.m. on December 31st, and the doctor said, "Don't feed him anything. He is not digesting it, and the bowels are not moving." My whole life, I didn't know there was anything called an IO. The doctor went ahead and said just prepare him for surgery. He couldn't eat or drink anything. I worried for my son, and a cold shiver ran down my body. At that moment, I could feel my mind and body saying we were tired of bad news and being under pressure all the time. But I had to be strong for my little man.

I was quiet; I didn't know what to do. Fortunately, all this happened while my brothers and sisters were with me in the hospital because I needed attention. In as much as I was strong for my son, I was physically, mentally, emotionally, and financially drained. In the beginning, my mom was with us, but time came, and she couldn't stay longer. She had to go back and see Dad. Dad needed her, but she was present on the phone all the time, so I called them, and both Dad and Mom encouraged me. They prayed for my son right after hearing that news, and all the rest of the family members started praying, and all our pastors started praying and speaking life to that situation.

The doctor called for a pediatric specialist surgeon, and he said he would come by 6 p.m. that day to have surgery. He gave instructions to prep me and my son for the procedure.

Meanwhile, my son was still in terrible pain. He had cried so much that he lost his voice, and he also didn't have tears anymore. I was in so much despair... as a mom, I didn't know what to do to help him. He looked at me as he cried, but I wasn't able to help. I couldn't bear it, so I handed my son over to my sister to hold, and I walked to a corner in the side of the room where I sat down. I didn't know how to pray anymore or what to say, so I said a prayer, shedding tears to God and asking him for another miracle. I reminded him of how he blessed me with my son, and I prayed for healing, mercy, and life over the situation he was going through. Trust me, there are some scenarios that just leave us tongue-tied sometimes, and this was it for me, but I needed to be strong and fight for my son, so I spoke life to his body, healing, and then started singing worship songs to God.

Soon, the nurses came by and said to dress my son up as it was time to go to the theatre. But as I was still trying to dress him up, one nurse came by and said the surgeon was held up. He says to monitor how my son is doing tonight, and he will be here first thing in the morning.

Now, with that being said, it was night shift, and a different doctor was coming in. The daytime one's shift was over with no change in my son's circumstance, so I said, "Lord, I know you are at work, as everything works together for the good of those who love you." Then I surrendered, but as soon as I said those prayers, the night shift pediatric specialist doctor came by and tried to move the tube in his mouth around so that it drains stuff from his tummy, and indeed, I saw stuff coming out from the tube! Quite a lot of what was causing him the distension started to drain out! I said, "Lord, thank you!" This was only God! Earlier on, when this was inserted, it didn't drain anything! But God was at work now!

And there was hope. That was all we needed, and my son was still crying and in pain, but not as much as he was. He had been in this pain for the whole day and night. I had checked his diapers, and there was still nothing—no poop or anything.

At 6 a.m. on January 1st, a nurse came by and said to get my son ready to go to the theatre for surgery, as the surgeon was here in the hospital that night, and we all had not slept in our family. We prayed for God's touch and miracle for my son so that he would recover from that IO, and I had been checking his diaper all this while, but there was nothing. However, that morning at 6:30 a.m., before he was rolled to the theatre, I decided to check his diaper again, and what I saw… up to now still amazes me at how God comes through for us! In the nick of time! There was a little bit of greenish poop in his diaper! I have never been so happy about seeing poop as that day! I got that diaper and jumped up, thanking God, looking at it and my son and my siblings, and just so excited at what God had done!! I mean, there was very little drainage, but at least that was a good sign! That God heard our cry, and the bowels moved! This was only God! I told the nurse and the doctor on duty, and they all were happy. They said this is a good sign! They informed the surgeon about it while waiting in the operating room, and he asked them to hold on before taking my son to the theatre so he could come and see the situation at bedside.

When the surgeon came by at 7 a.m., he looked at the diaper that I was holding like a golden prize, and he said, "This is a good sign! This child is lucky. Usually, nothing like this happens to his schedule. When it's an emergency surgery on a premie, he is on it, but he just couldn't get here on time yesterday. And also, for his bowels to start moving again by themselves was only God!"

He said no to the surgery. He asked the doctor in charge to monitor him for a couple of hours and keep him posted.

I kept holding my son, thanking God for his miracle, and just trusting for more miracles for the day. Finally, he slept after many hours of crying, and I got time to freshen up and just sing more worship songs as I waited.

At exactly 10 a.m., I went back to check his diaper as he was really sleeping, and his tummy seemed less distended. My brothers and sisters were resting too. As soon as I opened it, my goodness! There was a lot more poop! It was a miracle indeed! More came out! And, like I said, I had never ever been super excited at the sight of poop like I was that day! I mean, it wasn't like regular poop as he wasn't on solids yet, and it didn't have any foul smell, but I was excited! I cleaned him and changed him quick, then held on to the diaper.

I called the doctor and the nurses to see what God had done again. It was really needed, and he came through in a timely manner! We all celebrated the goodness of God and the miracle he had just done, healing my son and delivering him from surgery just on time. Trust me, that January 1st miracle was a true example of how our God cares, and when we ask him and wait, he delivers us miraculously. My son slept more that morning, and the doctor said I could nurse him when he wakes up. I also finally rested. We all hadn't eaten or slept. We started our new year in victory and amazement.

In as much as we were in the hospital, the peace of the Lord engulfed us, and we didn't care about what comes with celebrating New Year's Day. We were the most blessed and happiest with what God had just done for us. As the day progressed, there was more bowel movement, and everything started getting back to normal. His distended tummy went down, and the pain left.

I never saw the pediatric surgeon again that day. They took off the theatre outfit from him, and we continued our regular routine.

After one week, we were discharged to go home, where we kept on monitoring him and just praying for him. He still was sick here and there.

Just after 2 weeks home, he made 3 months, but his tummy seemed disturbed a lot from the effect of the IO he had. His food absorption and digestion were so bad that he got 3 more IOs, which were painful still, but with prayer and patience, they dissolved without surgery. However, this was causing problems in his tummy. He couldn't tolerate anything. Even when I nursed him, he passed stool instantly, and it smelt like milk.

He lost so much weight, the sepsis came back, and he seemed pale again. So I went back to the hospital, and he was sent back to the NICU in a different unit. He had his side head shaved off so a cannula could be put in for treatment, since all his feet and hand veins were exhausted by now. It seemed like we were moving backward, but we met a lady who was really nice. Her name was Miriam. She said my son would be well. She came and visited us with her husband Simon and son Darnel. We became friends and encouraged each other, as her son too was born before the due date. And indeed, my son got better. We were discharged and went back home.

Just a few weeks home, one day, I was changing his diaper, and I noticed a swelling on the side between his legs close to his groin. I got scared, and then I called his doctor, and she told me to bring him in. I went to the hospital, and the doctor said he had developed a groinal hernia and needed surgery right away. It was an emergency, and because that can be dangerous, as a matter of fact, she picked up the phone and called the pediatric surgeon, who said he wanted me to bring him in as soon as possible for surgery. I was so scared and worried for my boy. I remember crying to God for mercy and healing for him. My family prayed, and we said, "Lord, you didn't bring him this far to leave him. You preserved him from that IO that needed surgery. Please help him heal from this as well." I spoke Philippians 1:6, which says, "He that started a great thing in you shall bring it to accomplishment." I said this over his life all the time.

While trusting God, I went ahead and scheduled a date for the operation, but before going for it, I went to a different pediatric surgeon to hear his view on it. He said to wait it out, and if it didn't heal in 3 months, then he would need surgery.

And I really thanked God for giving me the wisdom to see this surgeon. So, I called and canceled the other appointment. And that groinal hernia disappeared that week. It never came back ever again, so yes, before 3 months, the groinal hernia was completely healed. Amen.

Time was up for a visit to the heart specialist to review his condition or do surgery.

When I went to see the heart specialist, it was the same one that saw us when my son was very weak and almost getting heart failure.

This time around, when she saw his heart, she jumped up off her seat and said, "Is this the same patient that came in with an ambulance and was almost having heart failure?" I said yes, and she said there was completely nothing wrong with his heart. He has no PDA. The hole is completely gone, and the heart is well developed. She again asked if this was the same child as the previous check. I said yes, and she was blown away at the goodness of God and how God had healed my son. Indeed, she said it must be God. Just God... I said yes, it is God. Amen.

And he was completely healed from anemia, healed from heart failure, healed from a heart defect, healed from infections, survived an emergency surgery, healed from an intestinal obstruction, healed from a groinal hernia.

Delay in Growth and Development

After all the heavy medications and the IO, my son's tummy was highly disturbed, and by 4 months, he had so much trouble keeping anything in his bowels. It was so bad that as soon as I fed him, he went number 2 right away, and it smelt like milk as he was still nursing exclusively. He couldn't contain any formula. It made his tummy sick, and he would cry straight up. This made him not add weight at all. He was not growing well. He looked smaller and was doing fewer activities than a child his age would be doing. He also was not sleeping at all. He slept for 2 hours most of the night and cried consistently every night for hours, so I would sit up the whole night trying to soothe him.

This happened for a whole year, and in all this, while I went back so many times to see his doctor, they couldn't diagnose anything wrong with his tummy. I went to all sorts of the best pediatric specialists in the city of Uganda and didn't find any solution for his condition. They did all sorts of checks, barium swallow, enema, or whatever tests were needed for the digestive system, and nothing. I saw the doctor that handled him in the NICU. She was a premie specialist, the only one in the country, but she still couldn't diagnose anything. I went to the most expensive hospitals in the city and still no solution.

All I did was continue praying for him as we had already done the whole time. I took him to church all the time. It was tough for us. He was weak all the time. This whole situation made me nervous, and

I developed anxiety because I was dealing with the emotional torture and worry all by myself. I was so tired I couldn't do anything else or leave his side. He needed my attention 100% all the time, as he was still frail, cranky, and hungry all the time. I had tried everything, and nothing seemed to work. When you see him, you would think he really was struggling with a condition affecting his thriving and growth. By the time he was 1 year old, that's when I realized he was still fitting in the same 6-month-old baby clothes. He was not crawling, sitting by himself, talking, or eating solids, and we were not sleeping at all.

I tried to feed him some egg and mashed potato when he was 9 months old, and he had a bad allergic reaction. He was throwing up unstoppably and crying, and I rushed him to the hospital. I ruled out the egg and feared feeding him. He also refused to eat solids again, as the egg and mashed potato were the first things he ate, and he had a bad reaction.

When he was one year old, my husband came by to see us and brought lots of gifts. He had been away for a whole year, and he flew in to see us briefly as he had a connecting flight to another country that same day. He held my son for a bit, and things just seemed off. My son didn't know him. Me and him had a disconnect. There was no future.

Jesus is the only Hope, Savior, and Healer.

While still struggling with my son's health, we moved to NY. Everything was different. From having my own big home to a completely different place. I had maids that helped at home, but in NY, it was a do-it-yourself thing. The health systems work differently, so I couldn't just see a pediatrician without an appointment, despite all the health challenges my son had. Gladly, a few months down the road, we managed to get an appointment with a good, highly recommended pediatric specialist in the city. I was so excited, hoping that finally, he could figure out a way to solve all my son's health problems.

We went for his visit. The doctor ran all his tests, checked him, did X-rays and ultrasounds, and still found nothing!

This was in December, a couple of months after my son's birthday. Looking at his age, the doctor acknowledged that the child needs to grow and add weight. He gave him no medication. Despite all the worry and concerns I had, I was puzzled, and I just knew, like I always know and my parents always tell us, it is only God that can heal, rescue, and deliver my son and anyone. I spoke Psalms 91 over his life every second. I spoke Psalms 23, Isaiah 53:5, Exodus 23:26, 1 Peter 2:24, and all the different scriptures. I anointed him and just kept on praying for him with my family and the pastors we knew all the time. I made a promise to God. I said, "Lord, if you heal my son, we will go all over the world and tell of your mighty works."

But the child was still stagnant in growth, cried every night consistently, and was still struggling to sit by himself unless supported. Not even moving. It seemed like God was far away, yet he was near.

To be honest, by this time, I was so tired. If anyone asked me my wish or prayer requests, I would say, "To sleep." I hadn't slept for more than 1 hour for a whole year ever since I had delivered him. Not even for 2 hours straight. The most I slept was 1 hour before I was woken up with a cry from my son. And I was alone, so even when my son slept for 2 hours (because that was the most he slept anyway), I would be cleaning or running to shower. And I hurriedly ran back from the shower when he was crying. I didn't do anything or go to anything fun. I was so depressed and taking care of him full time.

Christmas came, and I was asked what present I wanted. I said, "Sleep, for both me and my son." It had become a big deal.

One day, I was asked if he could be allergic to some things I was eating. I was still nursing him, and that's when I remembered the egg allergy reaction he had in Uganda. So I stopped eating eggs, and then I stopped eating dairy and anything that triggered his health.

New Year's Sleep Answered Prayer.

A few days into the New Year, we slept for 6 hours straight for the very first time since my son was born, and this was a miracle! A big one!

So I started eliminating from my diet anything I ate, and my son cried after nursing. I ended up eating a few foods, and I was so hungry, but I couldn't trade that with sleep! We were sleeping at least 6 hours or more straight! I took him to the hospital only once for immunization, and that was it.

I noticed his poop also became normal, not as runny and smelly as it was.

He started looking stronger. His hair started growing, and I noticed he kicked his feet more and was more vocal. All the while, he used to only cry and be quiet. Now, he was vocally playing and making sounds.

One day, I was in the kitchen. I usually left him on a little child rocker. He would be on that rocker in the living room, watching for hours. If I was busy in the kitchen until I picked him up to feed, he would be there. But on this day, I heard my sister's friend's son saying, "He is moving. The baby is moving." I looked back and saw my son in the kitchen where I was. He wasn't crawling, but he was somehow moving on his butt.

Oh my God! I was so happy I knelt down to thank God, and I

was in tears at the goodness of God and for answering our prayers.

Fast forward, my son healed completely. He started crawling and moving on his knees by 2 years and 7 months, then he started walking at 2 years and 9 months. But he was so weak, he tripped all the time but kept going. He then started learning how to speak.

Early Intervention

His doctor recommended early intervention and followed up with them. They did the evaluation, and he was approved to get physical therapy, speech, occupational, and other treatment. They got him to an Early Children Development Center School in NJ, where we lived at the time.

While he went to school, I realized that I could rest, pray, thank God, and sleep more. I was also being rehabilitated. I started looking at the goodness of God and how he made a way where there seemed to be no way.

How he protected my son and healed him made him whole.

He protected my heart, emotions, and health.

My son is now in a regular school, and he is doing well.

We all need healing from something in one way or another. Our struggles are completely different. It could be a need for emotional, mental, financial, or physical healing. My dear, keep up the faith. Trust that someday all will be well. Don't give up. Look up to God and surrender.

He is a God that does wonders. Don't give up on that situation, my sisters and brothers. Be encouraged, pray without ceasing, read the word of the Lord, forgive, and surrender to him, and he will come through in a mighty way.

Now, if this story touched you and you still haven't given your life to Jesus, and you want him to work in your life and be your Lord and Savior, your healer, please say these words:

"Dear God, thank you for my life, thank you for this opportunity. I ask that you come into my life and be my Lord and Savior, forgive all my sins, make me whole again, and cleanse me with your precious blood. I receive you in my life to be my Lord and Savior, write my name in the book of life in Jesus's mighty name. Amen"

Now, my friend, find a nearby church and get plugged in. See the goodness of the Lord in your life!

Back to my son, he is now grown so big and taller than all his age mates. He is completely 100% healed from everything. He didn't have any surgery at all, and all of this by God's grace.

Thanks to Dad, Mom, all my siblings, pastors, friends, and relatives who never gave up and never stopped praying for us. We love you.

All the glory goes back to God! Amen.

I leave you with Psalms 91.

And God has got you!

God bless…

How to heal from a loss:

1. Accept that it happened

2. Grieve and cry

3. Don't isolate yourself

4. Don't blame yourself or the situation

5. Surrender to God

6. Ask God to heal you

7. Talk about it

8. Read about it

9. Take each day at a time

10. Move forward and try again

How to build your faith and trust God amidst difficulty:

1. Read the bible

2. Sync God's word with that situation

3. Speak hope and life through that season

4. Pray without ceasing

5. Don't give up

6. Find a church community

7. Talk about your challenges

8. Be positive, keep going

9. Celebrate your harvest

10. Testify!

Amen.

Healed from a long-term gastrointestinal condition

Healed from sleeplessness

Started moving

Sit

Crawl

Walk

Run

Started speaking

Improved speech

Healed from allergies and all the glory goes back to God

Amen

Note to Readers

I pray this book encourages you and helps you heal in all ways. My case was different; yours could be different, and once you surrender it to God, you will be liberated. The peace that will come over you is amazing.

Also, he may answer you differently, but remember that God has a great plan for your life. Be content with whatever direction he leads you through your journey, for all things work together for the good of those who love him. Amen.

About the Author

I grew up very enthusiastic about life and in a Christian home. Dad and Mom prayed with us every night. Somehow, I thought I had to be a Christian because I was obliged to. So, that mindset caused me to stray away at some point. However, with all my experiences, I sought God by myself, not because my mom or dad wanted me to. I love God so much, and I am so glad for salvation and for Jesus.

I love writing and singing.

And I fell in love with loving God.